AF413271

# THE
# STORM
# PLAN

# THE
# STORM
# PLAN

A Tiny Book for Busy Parents Who
Struggle with Their Child's Behavior
and Are Ready for More Peace

LAURA REARDON

Library of Congress Control Number: 2025903834

ISBN (Hardback): 979-8-218-77047-1
ISBN (Ebook): 979-8-218-77048-8

Published by Laura Reardon Coaching
Massachusetts USA
www.laurareardoncoaching.com

**For my son and daughter, who are my sun and moon.**

I couldn't feel prouder to be your mom
and I couldn't love you more.

# Contents

# Preface

**As a mom, I struggled to create peace in my family.**

Over time, I came to understand that nervous system regulation is the foundation of behavior—but I couldn't find a parenting resource that offered a complete plan for my family: one that helped me regulate my own nervous system while also supporting my individual children in regulating theirs.

**Inspired by the desire to create more peace in my own family—and to help other parents do the same—I spent five years researching and writing _The Storm Plan_.**

_The Storm Plan_ is a practical, two-part framework designed to help you regulate your unique nervous system and support your children in regulating theirs—so you can show up as the parent you aspire to be and bring out the best in each child, creating more peace in your family.

From there, I created The CUSTOMIZED Storm Plan to help parents personalize _The Storm Plan_ to meet their family's individual needs and support them as they practice using it.

**My training and experience include:**

- Child Behavior Coach certification with The Early Years

- Parent Coach training with Happily Family
- Nervous System Regulation training with The Brain-Body Parenting Collective
- Emotion Coach training with The Gottman Institute
- Childhood Anxiety training with the Institute of Child Psychology
- Conflict Resolution training with The Gottman Institute
- The Wayfinder's Compass training with Martha Beck
- Degree in psychology from Northeastern University
- Two decades of experience working as a mom, licensed home daycare provider, and professional nanny

**I'm not here to tell you how to parent.** I'm here to share a plan for nervous system regulation so you can create more peace in your family. And so your children can grow up to be adults who know how to create peace within themselves, in their relationships, and in the world around them.

# SECTION 1

# How Storms Form

# Weather 101

Parents, are you ready for more peace?

More peace in your family begins with understanding why nervous system regulation is the foundation of behavior.

Our nervous system facilitates the exchange of information between our brain and our body, and its primary job is to use that information to keep us safe.

This is how it works:

**We experience our world through sensations.**

1. <u>Internal sensations</u>: sensations inside our body such as hungry or full, thirsty or not, energized or tired, warm or cold, light or heavy. We might also feel pressure or no pressure, relaxed or tense, in pain or comfortable, or notice our heart beating slowly or quickly.
2. <u>External sensations</u>: what we hear, see, smell, taste, touch.
3. <u>Relationship sensations</u>: felt signals we experience in response to body language—both our own and that of

others. These include tone of voice, facial expressions, posture, movement, and gestures.

**This sensory data is sent to our brain which automatically and subconsciously perceives safety or threat based on our past experiences with similar sensations.** Steven Porges, PhD, author of *The Polyvagal Theory*, coined the term "neuroception" to describe this process.

**When our brain perceives safety or manageable threat,** it activates a state of nervous system regulation and we instinctively respond as our best self.

I define our "best self" as Richard Schwartz, PhD, author of *Internal Family Systems,* defines "The Self." When we act as our best self, we display qualities of the 8 Cs and 5 Ps:

- 8 Cs – Confidence, Calmness, Creativity, Clarity, Curiosity, Courage, Compassion, Connectedness
- 5 Ps – Presence, Patience, Perspective, Persistence, Playfulness

**When our brain perceives too much threat,** it triggers a state of nervous system <u>dys</u>regulation to prepare our body to defend itself and we instinctively react as our defensive self.

Nervous system dysregulation is a deeply rooted survival instinct that has helped humans react quickly to danger since we first evolved.

In modern life, however, nervous system dysregulation is more often triggered by too much stress caused by everyday challenges rather than too much threat caused by physical danger.

> When we experience too much stress, it triggers nervous system <u>dys</u>regulation, and our instinct is to react as our defensive self.

## FOR EXAMPLE:

<u>When a younger child</u> needs to move their body, but is expected to stay still; doesn't like the taste of their food, but we're insisting they finish it; wants our attention, but we're feeding the baby; is playing with a toy and another child grabs it from them, or must transition from one activity to another when they're not ready to...

<u>When an older child</u> gets home from school and is on empty; is immersed in a video game, and we ask them to turn it off; is hungry, but dinner isn't ready yet; is tired but is expected to do their homework; or is stressed because of their test/performance/game the next day...

<u>As a parent,</u> when our older child starts yelling right after we got the baby to sleep; we feel overwhelmed by constant touch; are trying to work, and they keep interrupting us; they're late getting ready for school; we ask them to turn off their iPad and they react disrespectfully; or we're tired and they're late getting home...

One or, more often, a combination of these everyday challenges can create too much stress and trigger nervous system dysregulation. Our instinct is to react as our defensive self rather than as our best self:

- Fight – lash out with our body or our words
- Flight – withdraw physically
- Freeze – withdraw emotionally
- Fawn – people-please to avoid conflict

And for people—adults and children alike—who are deeply feeling, sensory sensitive, have ADHD, ASD, have experienced trauma, or have other individual differences, they may experience things more intensely, so their nervous system can get dysregulated more easily.

> When we keep our stress in check, it activates nervous system regulation, and our instinct is to respond as our best self.

**My definition of peace is the ability to remain in a state of nervous system regulation—even when faced with too much stress—so we can respond to everyday challenges as our best self rather than react as our defensive self.**

*The Storm Plan* is a practical, two-part framework designed to help you regulate your unique nervous system and support your children in regulating theirs—so you can show up as the parent you aspire to be and bring out the best in each child, creating more peace in your family.

# SECTION 2

# Your Storm Plan

# An Introduction

As parents, when we react to everyday challenges in a defensive way, our stormy behavior can look like:

- <u>Lashing out</u>: Yelling, criticizing, interrupting, shaming, threatening, overreacting with harsh consequences, or interacting with our child in a forceful way.
- <u>Withdrawing</u>: Storming away or ignoring our child.
- <u>People-pleasing</u>: Letting go of boundaries, taking responsibility for our child's responsibilities, or avoiding difficult conversations.

**We can recognize our stormy behavior as an instinctive reaction to too much stress while also recognizing that reacting to our child in a stormy way is not effective because...**

**It fuels our child's stress:**

- <u>If we lash out</u>, it fuels their stress because they need us to stay calm so they can feel safe.
- <u>If we withdraw physically or emotionally</u>, it fuels their

stress because they need a connection with us to feel safe.

- <u>If we appease</u>, it fuels their stress because they need us to be "the captain of the ship" to feel safe (Susan Stiffelman, author of *Parenting Without Power Struggles*).

**And when we fuel their stress, we fuel their stormy behavior:**

- <u>If your child reacts by fawning</u>, defensive parenting can appear to be effective on the surface, but fawning is a stress response.
- <u>If your child reacts by lashing out or withdrawing,</u> they will make it clear to you that defensive parenting only serves to escalate their stormy behavior.

**Either way, a pattern of defensive parenting can lead to the chronic activation of stress in our child, which negatively impacts:**

- Physical well-being
- Emotional well-being
- Relationship with self and others

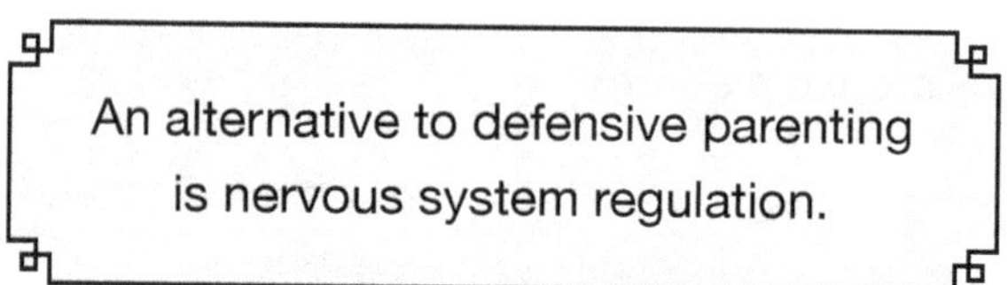


Nervous system regulation requires a combination of brain

development and skills. As parents, we may have a fully developed brain, but many of us were never taught the skills. Thanks to neuroplasticity (the brain's ability to change in response to new experiences), it's never too late to learn new skills so you can show up as the parent you aspire to be.

# When Skies are Clear

**We want to allow ourselves to experience manageable stress** caused by everyday challenges because when we stretch ourselves outside of our comfort zone, we...

- build our tolerance for stress.
- learn and grow into our best selves.

**However,** an experience that fuels manageable stress in one parent may fuel too much stress in another based on individual differences such as genetics and past experiences.

Too much stress can lead to dysregulation—shutting down our capacity to learn and grow and triggering our instinct to react defensively. Therefore, we want to keep our stress in check.

> Tune in and respond to your needs
> to keep your stress in check.

**It's not about tuning in and responding to every need.** It's about creating a balance that allows us to experience manageable stress so we can build tolerance for it, learn, and grow—while also tuning in and responding to our needs, because:

- Unmet needs can fuel stress and lead to dysregulation, and dysregulation promotes more dysregulation—a vicious cycle,
- Whereas met needs can fuel safety and lead to regulation, and regulation promotes more regulation—a virtuous cycle.

**These are some of our needs that, when met, keep our stress in check and support regulation.**

- <u>Physiological needs</u>: physical safety and well-being, sleep, nutrition, hydration, movement, sensory comfort, and downtime.
- <u>Psychological needs</u>: emotional safety and well-being, connection (feeling connected to others, yourself, and nature), play, predictability, novelty, autonomy, respect, recognition, personal space, intellectual stimulation, a sense of purpose, and spirituality, as well as <u>less</u> screen time, busyness, news, and negativity.

**We can recognize our individual needs by noticing the clues our body and brain are sending.** The <u>pleasant</u> sensations we experience, thoughts we have, and emotions we feel communicate met needs, whereas <u>unpleasant</u> ones communicate unmet needs.

**When we experience discomfort,** we can practice staying present with an attitude of curiosity about what we need to support our well-being—rather than ignoring it, minimizing it, or rushing to get rid of it.

## SENSATIONS

**Internal, external, and relationship sensations communicate information about our needs.** For example, a rumbling stomach may be a clue to a need for nutrition, experiencing a sensation in our ears that signals the noise is too loud may be a clue that we need sensory comfort, and experiencing a felt sense of safety from another person may be a clue to a met need for connection with others.

**Our body sensations can also communicate information about the emotions we're experiencing, which serve as a clue to our needs.**

- Clenched muscles in your jaw, fists, and shoulders together with a feeling of heat in your body may be a clue to anger and a need for respect.
- A feeling of tightness in your stomach or chest may be a clue to anxious feelings and a need for emotional well-being.
- A feeling of lightness in your body may be a clue to joy and a met need for novelty.

According to occupational therapist, Kelly Mahler, tuning in with our body to know our needs is the foundation of mental health and well-being. Unfortunately, there is no chart we can look at to know what our sensations mean. This is because we all feel our own unique sensations and they mean their own unique things, so it's a matter of getting to know your individual self.

# THOUGHTS

**Thoughts are the words or images we experience in response to what's happening inside us and around us…but thoughts are not facts.** "Thoughts are subjective interpretations of events based on our personal experiences, biases, and perspectives and not necessarily the truth itself." (Daniel Siegel, MD, author of *Aware*). Therefore, we can respond to our thoughts with curiosity about whether they are true or not true to know our needs.

An effective way to question our thoughts is to do *The Work* (Byron Katie, author of *Loving What Is).*

For example, if you think, "I'm a bad parent," you can question that thought:

- Is it true?
- Can you absolutely know that it's true?
- How do you feel and act when you have that thought?
- How would you feel and act without that thought?
- Could the opposite thought be true?
- Could the opposite thought be truer than your original thought?

# EMOTIONS

**Emotions are the feelings we experience in response to what's happening inside us and around us.**

People who feel their emotions more deeply may sometimes think that those who feel them more subtly are insensitive or suppressing their emotions. On the other hand, those who experience emotions more subtly may view those who feel them more deeply as overly sensitive. In reality, how we experience emotions is influenced by our genetics and past experiences, making each person's emotional experience unique and valid.

For someone who feels their emotions more deeply, this can lead to greater emotional insight, stronger relationships, and personal growth. For someone who feels emotions more subtly, it may be easier to stay calm and level-headed in tough situations. That said, if your emotions regularly feel too intense or too numb, it can be hard to tune into them as a clue to your needs. In those cases, it may be helpful to explore what would support your ability to experience your emotions in a connected way.

**The goal is to tune in with your natural emotional response and then practice staying present with an attitude of curiosity about what it's communicating about your needs.** For example, if you feel sad, you may need a safe space to grieve—whether that's with yourself, with others, or in nature. If you feel overwhelmed, you may need predictability or downtime. If you feel bored, you may need intellectual stimulation or a sense of purpose.

**Body sensations, thoughts, and emotions form an interconnected feedback loop.** Understanding this connection helps us respond with more awareness, which supports our ability to recognize our needs and take action to meet them—supporting regulation.

- A thought can trigger emotional and physical responses.
- An emotion can bring up specific thoughts or bodily sensations.
- A physical sensation can influence how we think and feel.

**If we notice unpleasant sensations, thoughts, or emotions but don't know what they communicate about our needs,** we can simply allow them to exist while remaining curious. By allowing them to exist without immediately reacting, we can take the time we need to better understand our needs.

**For support in tuning into our body and brain,** we can use the *Wheel of Awareness* meditation, designed to enhance self-awareness. First introduced in *The Whole-Brain Child* by Daniel J. Siegel, MD, and Tina Payne Bryson, PhD, it's available for free at drdanielsiegel.com. And then we can practice checking in with ourselves in small moments throughout the day—like when we're in the car waiting for our child, or taking a break from the screen at work. In those moments, we can notice our sensations, thoughts, and emotions.

**Once we tune in with a need, we can respond by meeting it or by helping ourselves tolerate one that cannot be met.**

<u>Prioritize primary needs</u>: As parents, it can be very challenging to meet our needs at a time when we're also responsible for the needs of our child. We can set ourselves up for success by doing our best to prioritize our primary needs for things such as sleep, nutrition, movement, and connection—with others, ourselves, and nature. We can think of meeting our primary needs as wrapping ourselves in a "sanity quilt" (Martha Beck, PhD, author of *Beyond Anxiety*). Beck teaches that when we create our sanity quilt, we put the thing that is most fundamental in supporting our well-being in the center. Then you can stitch in patches around it that also contribute to your well-being to create a sanity quilt that is uniquely yours. And then you can do what you need to create enough sanity in your life, whether that is snuggling up with your kids and watching a good movie so you can have a rest, sneaking to the bathroom so you can have a moment alone, or hiring a babysitter so you can get out with other adults.

<u>If we know what we need but don't know how to meet the need</u>, we can tap into the Eureka effect named after the Greek mathematician Archimedes and referenced in a book called Borrowing Brilliance by David Kord Murray. Here's how to do it:

- Identify the problem you want to solve.
- Think deeply about a solution until you reach a stuck point.
- Stop giving the problem your attention and go do something unrelated.

When you give a problem your full attention and then walk

away from it, "the solution can present itself in your mind" (Martha Beck, PhD, The Wayfinders Compass training).

<u>Tolerate unmet needs</u>: Some needs simply can't be met in the moment or at all. For example, a parent of a younger child may experience an unmet need for enough alone time. A parent of an older child may experience an unmet need for predictability as their child becomes more independent. Part of nervous system regulation is learning how to tolerate unmet needs (which will be covered in detail in the next section).

**If we need something from someone else, we can communicate our needs.**

<u>If we communicate ineffectively</u>, we set ourselves up to fail in getting our needs met because the other person may feel attacked, which is likely to trigger a defensive reaction. When this happens, it can cause endless arguments that waste a great deal of energy and only serve to escalate our stress rather than reduce it. Some examples of ineffective communication habits include:

- Raising your voice or using a sharp, harsh, or aggressive tone
- Using language that blames, shames, or threatens
- Making demands rather than requests

The Four Horsemen are four ineffective communication habits identified as strong predictors of relationship breakdown (John and Julie Gottman, PhD's, authors of Fight Right).

- <u>Criticism</u>: Attacking your partner's character or

personality instead of focusing on a specific behavior. For example, "You never think about anyone but yourself."

- <u>Contempt</u>: Showing disrespect, sarcasm, mockery, eye-rolling, or name-calling. For example, "Oh please, like you even know what you're talking about." This is the most destructive of the four.
- <u>Defensiveness</u>: Playing the victim or blaming your partner to avoid taking responsibility. For example, "It's not my fault! You're the one who always starts it."
- <u>Stonewalling</u>: Withdrawing, shutting down, or refusing to engage during conflict. For example: Giving your partner the silent treatment or walking away mid-conversation without explanation.

<u>If we communicate effectively</u>, we set ourselves up for success in getting our needs met because it keeps the other person's defenses down and open to responding as their best self. *Nonviolent Communication*, developed by Marshall Rosenberg, is a communication style that promotes effective problem-solving through four key steps:

1. **When** _____: State what you see, hear, or experience without judgment.
2. **I feel** _____: Identify and express your emotional response to the situation being careful to distinguish between feelings and thoughts. For example, say "I feel frustrated" rather than "I think you're being disrespectful."

3. **Because my need for _____ is not met**: Connect your feelings to the underlying needs that are not being met.
4. **Would you be willing to _____?**: Ask for specific, positive actions that would meet your needs.

<u>In your relationship with your parenting partner, this could sound like</u>:

- When I see dishes in the sink after I come down from putting the kids to bed, I feel frustrated because my need for downtime is not being met. Could we make a plan to share the chores more evenly?
- When we don't schedule time for just the two of us, I feel lonely because my need for connection is not being met. Could we schedule a date-night?
- When you make a purchase I'm not expecting, I feel anxious because my need for predictability is not being met. Could we agree to discuss purchases over a certain dollar amount before making them?

<u>If your partner expresses their own feelings and needs</u>, "What's a solution that would work for both of us?

<u>But the reality is that most people struggle to identify their emotions.</u> If you struggle to name your emotions, you are not alone. Marc Brackett, PhD, is the founding director of the Yale Center for Emotional Intelligence and author of *Permission to Feel*. Brackett's research shows that most people, from preschoolers to CEO's, are unable to identify their emotions.

Brackett developed a Mood Meter and a corresponding emotion word list to help people learn to identify and communicate their emotions. The Mood Meter is a grid that organizes emotions along two axes:

- Energy (high to low)
- Pleasantness (pleasant to unpleasant)

Each quadrant of the Mood Meter represents a different emotional state.

<u>Unpleasant with High Energy</u>
You may feel:
- Angry
- Anxious
- Frustrated
- Impatient
- Worried

<u>Unpleasant with Low Energy</u>
You may feel:
- Sad
- Disappointed
- Lonely
- Discouraged
- Tired

<u>Pleasant with Low Energy</u>
You may feel:
- Calm
- Content
- Peaceful
- Grateful
- Comfortable

<u>Pleasant with High Energy</u>

You may feel:

- Excited
- Joyful
- Inspired
- Motivated
- Hopeful

**As we begin developing awareness of our own feelings and needs, we begin to have more awareness of the feelings and needs of others.**

# When a Storm is Brewing

> Notice when your stress gets close to the line (or crosses it) and hold boundaries on your behavior while taking action to lower your stress.

**Turn stormy behavior into best behavior:** Noticing too much stress and lowering it isn't about shielding ourselves from discomfort. It's about sensing when our stress gets close to the line (or crosses it)—the line between manageable stress, which builds tolerance, learning, and growth, and too much stress, which leads to dysregulation.

When we sense that our stress is close to the line (or has crossed it), we can hold boundaries of our behavior while taking action to lower our stress so we can stay regulated (or return to regulation in a triggered moment).

# NOTICE WHEN STRESS GETS CLOSE TO THE LINE (OR CROSSES IT)

Different parents have different stress thresholds.

When we experience stress, it can show up as unpleasant sensations, thoughts, or emotions. By checking in with our body and brain, we can notice these signals as clues to how close we are to our individual stress threshold.

**Clues that we are in a regulated state:**

- <u>Internal sensations</u>: relaxed muscles, a slow heart rate, and balanced energy—not sluggish or jittery
- <u>External sensations</u>: pleasant sensory input such as gentle sounds, soft lighting or calming visuals, comforting scents, soothing tastes, and warm or soft touch
- <u>Relationship sensations</u>: signals we send or receive that elicit connection, such as a soft or friendly tone of voice, a neutral expression or genuine smile, an open posture with arms by our sides or leaning slightly forward to show engagement, and calm movements
- <u>Thoughts</u>: thoughts that assume the best in ourselves and others
- <u>Emotions</u>: emotions that feel good, such as calm, contentment, or joy

**Clues that our stress may be building:**

- <u>Internal sensations</u>: a quickened heart rate, muscle tension, increased body temperature, tingling or numbness in the fingers, a clenched or queasy stomach, and sluggish or jittery energy

- <u>External sensations</u>: unpleasant sensory input such as loud noises, bright lights or overstimulating visuals, strong odors, off-putting flavors, or touch that feels overwhelming or uncomfortable
- <u>Relationship sensations</u>: signals we send or receive that create disconnection—such as a loud, sharp, or sarcastic tone of voice; a glaring look; avoiding eye contact; a furrowed brow and crossed arms; leaning too far forward in an aggressive way; and increased or decreased movement
- <u>Thoughts</u>: thoughts that assume the worst in ourselves or others
- <u>Emotions</u>: emotions that feel bad, such as anger, fear, or sadness

Once we have awareness, we have a choice, without awareness we do not.

## HOLD BOUNDARIES ON BEHAVIOR

As parents we can experience a lot of stress, so it's often our instinct to react to everyday challenges in a defensive way—raising our voice, saying things we don't mean, doing things we don't want to, or shutting down.

When we notice that our stress is close to the line (or has crossed it), we can choose to take intentional action to regulate our nervous system, so we can respond to everyday challenges as our best self rather than our defensive self.

"You don't have to attend every argument you're invited to" (Jefferson Fisher, author of *The Next Conversation*).

## TAKE ACTION TO LOWER STRESS

Lowering our stress supports our ability to stay regulated (or return to regulation in a triggered moment). We can lower our stress by meeting a need or tolerating an unmet need.

**Meet a need:**

Sometimes we can lower stress by identifying and meeting a need. Maybe we need a drink of water or something to eat. Maybe we need to dim the lights or reduce the noise. Maybe we need to set a boundary or step away to have a moment alone.

More often, we may not know what we need, or we may not be able to meet a need at that moment. For example, when our child unexpectedly has a meltdown, as parents, we may be experiencing a need for predictability—but that need can't be met right then.

When we don't know what our needs are, or we're unable to meet them, we can help ourselves tolerate an unmet need.

**Tolerate an unmet need:**

Unmet needs fuel stress. Stress fuels unpleasant sensations, thoughts, and emotions. Unpleasant sensations, thoughts, and emotions fuel more stress. More stress fuels unpleasant sensations, thoughts, and emotions. This is a feedback loop that supports dysregulation.

We can tolerate unmet needs without getting stuck in a feed-back loop by redirecting our focus to a sensation, thought, or emotion that fuels safety rather than stress. For example:

- Internal sensation: Take a deep breath in and a longer breath out.
- External sensation: Look at something in nature by stepping outside, looking out your window, or looking at your phone (take a video of a peaceful moment in nature and save it to your phone).
- Relationship sensation: Text a friend.
- Thought: Offer yourself compassion.
- Emotion: Focus on the feeling of kindness toward yourself or others.

**Based on genetics and past experiences, each person is unique in what strategies—or combinations of strategies—fuel safety versus stress.** What creates a sense of safety for one person may cause stress for another. There is no "right way" to reduce stress—only what works best for you and your specific situation. Consider the following ideas, along with your own, and then create a personalized list of strategies that resonate with you. Then visualize yourself using them. This way you will be prepared to take action when needed. If your attempt to help yourself reduce your stress causes it to escalate, try something different or ask yourself, "What would help me feel better in this moment?"

Depending on our level of stress, some strategies may help us tolerate an unmet need in a triggered moment, while others may be more effective in a calm moment at a later time.

## REDIRECT YOUR FOCUS TO AN
### *INTERNAL SENSATION*

**Mindful breathing**: Take a deep breath in through your nose, down into your belly, and let out a slow exhale through pursed lips that is longer than your inhale.

**Physiological sigh**: "A physiological sigh is the fastest, most robust way to calm our nervous system" (Andrew Huberman, PhD, host of *The Huberman Lab* podcast). It's a double inhale through the nose to maximally fill the lungs with air (the first inhale being a long one and the second inhale being a short one) followed by an extended exhale through the mouth to empty the lungs. If it's not possible to inhale through your nose, it's always ok to inhale through your mouth.

*Conversational Breath: Jefferson Fisher, author of *The Next Conversation*, coined the term Conversational Breath to describe the idea of using a physiological sigh to calm yourself without anyone realizing you're doing it. "Inject a sigh into your breath without it sounding like one." Fisher suggests an initial 2 second inhale, followed by an additional 1 second inhale, and then a 6 second exhale.

**Stop, breathe, be**: Stop, breathe, and ground your feet on the floor to connect with the present moment (Aditi Nerurkar, MD, author of *The 5 Resets*).

**Movement**: Stretch, sway from side to side, touch your toes, bounce on your tiptoes, run in place, shake your whole body, or get into a yoga pose.

**Progressive muscle relaxation**: Clench a muscle as you breathe in and release the tension all at once as you breathe out. If you want to be discreet, you can squeeze and release your toes.

## REDIRECT YOUR FOCUS TO AN
### *EXTERNAL SENSATION*

**Sight**: Look at something in nature by stepping outside, looking out your window, or looking at your phone (take a video of a peaceful moment in nature and save it to your phone); look at a picture in your home that evokes calm; look at a picture of a connected moment between you and your child (make it the wallpaper on your phone).

**Sound**: Play music you enjoy, use a sound machine to play a calming sound, or step outside and listen to the sounds of nature.

**Smell**: Smell an essential oil, spray room freshener, apply a scented lotion, light a candle, or turn on a diffuser.

**Taste**: Have a hot or cold drink, eat something with a texture that appeals—like crunchy or smooth, suck on a piece of hard candy, or chew some gum.

**Touch**: Hug yourself, wrap yourself in a cozy blanket, pat your pet. Run your hands under cold or warm water or splash some on your face. Feel the earth beneath your bare feet; feel the warmth of sunshine on your skin.

Other strategies include these by Nicole Lepera, PhD, author of *How to Do the Work* and the workbook *How to Meet Yourself.*

- <u>Cold exposure</u>: Place an ice pack or frozen veggies on the back of your neck for one to two minutes while breathing slowly and deeply.
- <u>Ear release</u>: Place your index finger inside your ear at the bottom and pull gently down and hold for about twenty seconds while breathing slowly and deeply. Check-in with yourself to notice if you feel calmer and then do it again with the other ear.
- <u>Bi-lateral stimulation</u>: Put your right hand on your left shoulder and your left hand on your right shoulder, then alternate gently tapping each shoulder in a consistent rhythm or pattern.
- <u>Tapping</u>: Gently tap the middle of your chest with two fingertips.

**Tune into all five senses**:

- What can you hear?
- What can you see?

- What can you smell?
- What can you taste?
- What can you feel on your skin?

## REDIRECT YOUR FOCUS TO A
### *RELATIONSHIP SENSATION*

<u>Use your body language to send yourself signals of safety.</u>

**Smile**, even if forced.

**Maintain a good posture** with a straight back and shoulders rolled back.

**Unfold your arms** and allow yourself to be open to the situation.

<u>Seek out signals of safety from others.</u>

**Reach out to another adult:** Text or call your partner, a friend, or a family member.

**Take the kids somewhere there will be other adults**, such as the library, a playground, the grocery store, or a coffee shop.

**Watch a show** together with your child.

**Listen to a podcast or read a book** if you can take a break.

# REDIRECT YOUR FOCUS TO A
## *THOUGHT OR EMOTION*

**Self-compassion:** "Instead of just ignoring your pain with a 'stiff upper lip' mentality or getting carried away by your negative thoughts and emotions, you stop to tell yourself, 'This is really difficult right now. How can I comfort and care for myself in this moment?'" (Kristin Neff, PhD, author of *Self-Compassion and Fierce Self-Compassion*)

**KIST:** Offer yourself kind internal self-talk (Martha Beck, PhD, author of *Beyond Anxiety).*

**Accept the moment as it is:** When we can accept the moment as it is, even when it's not what we want it to be, this is the necessary first step for connecting with our wisdom to know what to do next (Eckhart Tolle, author of *The Power of Now*).

**Thank the protective part of yourself:** "Thank you for protecting me, but I am safe."

**Mantra:**

- "This is an opportunity to practice regulating my nervous system."
- "How would my best self respond in this moment?"
- "I've got this."

**Change your thoughts**: When your thoughts assume the worst, change them to ones that assume the best, "My kid is a good kid who doesn't yet have the brain development and skills to respond to everyday challenges as their best self."

**Switch from judgment to curiosity:** "I wonder what's triggering my instinct to react defensively?"

**Change the story in your head:** For example, if you think "This is too hard," you can consider the opposite thought "I can do hard things" (Glennon Doyle, Abby Wambach, and Amanda Doyle, authors of *We Can Do Hard Things*).

**Think in verbs:** Focus on the action you want to take to show up the way you intend to (Jefferson Fisher, author of *The Next Conversation*). For example, you might say to yourself, "Listen without interrupting," or "Hold your boundary while allowing your child to disagree with it."

**Challenge negative self-talk:** Ask yourself what you would say to a friend in the same situation.

**If you're catastrophizing:** Consider this thought, "What if it all works out?" (Mel Robbins, author of *The Let Them Theory*).

**Let them and let me:** Think to yourself, "Let my child act like a child and let me respond with the support they need to learn and grow into their best self." (an implementation of *The Let Them Theory* by Mel Robbins).

**Re-imagine the past or future:** If you're feeling triggered by thoughts of regret about the past or worry about the future, shift your focus. Imagine the past unfolding exactly as you wish it had because our unconscious mind doesn't know the difference between memory and imagination. Or imagine your future unfolding exactly the way you want it to, making it more likely that you'll create the future you desire.

**Present moment gratitude:** Ask yourself, "What's happening right now that's good?"

**Let it stay:** "Respond to a negative emotion by saying 'Let it stay,' and it immediately starts to transmute into its opposite—so fear becomes courage, grief becomes compassion and joy, and anger becomes a way forward to justice" (Martha Beck, PhD, The Gathering Room podcast).

**Talk to your emotion:** "You're a part of me—but not all of me" (Becky Kennedy, PhD, author of *Good Inside*).

**Create distance between yourself and your emotions:** If at times we experience emotions that feel overwhelming, it may reduce our stress to let it all out. But sometimes, when we focus too much on our emotions, it fuels our stress. In these moments, creating distance between ourselves and our emotions can help. This is not about ignoring them. Ignoring them can leave us stuck in unpleasant emotions and unmet needs, fueling our stress and stormy behavior. Instead, it's about giving ourselves space to work through them in a way that feels more manageable.

- <u>Name your emotion</u>: "I feel _____."
- <u>Validate your emotion</u>: "It makes sense that I feel this way."

- <u>Remind yourself that emotions are temporary</u>: "I won't always feel this way."
- <u>Become curious</u>: "What would help me feel better in this moment?"

**Choose a different emotion:** Lisa Feldman Barrett, PhD, is among the top 0.1% most cited scientists in the world for her research in psychology and neuroscience and the author of *How Emotions Are Made*. Her research shows that our emotions are not facts but rather our mind's best guess about how we should feel in reaction to the sensations we're experiencing. Therefore, we have flexibility in how we feel. For example, if our mind guesses we feel anxious and that emotion only serves to fuel a feedback loop, we can make a different guess. We can choose an emotion that flips the feedback loop. We can guess that those sensations mean we feel excited or determined. "When we guess differently, we get our butterflies flying in the right direction" (Barrett). The larger our emotional vocabulary, the more flexible we can be in how we feel.

**Feel more than one emotion at a time:** Painful emotions such as sorrow, anger, and fear can coexist with the emotion of joy because, unlike happiness, which we only experience when good things happen, joy is something we can feel no matter what's happening. Joy is a quiet feeling deep inside that focuses on gratitude, awe, and a deep sense that everything will be okay. (Martha Beck, PhD, author of *Beyond Anxiety*)

**Kindness:** Focus on the feeling of kindness toward yourself and others.

**Visualization:**

- <u>Calm</u>: Bring to mind a pleasant image such as a calm ocean at sunset, a quiet forest path, a cozy fireplace, a flowing stream, a snowy winter landscape, a lush green meadow, majestic mountains, a floating cloud, a peaceful garden, a gentle rainfall, or a starry night.
- <u>Courage</u>: Bring to mind a time you acted with courage to reconnect with that emotion.
- <u>Joy</u>: Bring to mind a time you felt joy to reconnect with that emotion.

**Strategies from Marc Brackett, PhD, founding director of Yale's Center for Emotional Intelligence and author of *Permission to Feel.***

- <u>Feeling irritated</u>? Ask yourself if this is something that will bother you next week.
- <u>Feeling angry</u>? Put what's happening in a picture frame and pretend you're watching a show with an attitude of distanced curiosity rather than anger.
- <u>Feeling anxious</u>? Imagine yourself getting in a hot-air balloon and rising overhead to give yourself a new perspective.

**Here are some examples of how you can combine strategies to lower your stress:**

- Squeeze and then relax your toes—and then unfold

your arms and allow yourself to be open to the situation.

- Take a sip of water, and then say to yourself, "This is an opportunity to practice regulating my nervous system."
- Give your negative emotions permission to stay and then focus on gratitude (Martha Beck, PhD, Wayfinder Compass Training).
- Take a mindful breath and then offer yourself kind internal self-talk (Martha Beck, PhD, *Beyond Anxiety*).
- Take a conversational breath and then think in verbs, "I will listen without interrupting" (Jefferson Fisher, author of *The Next Conversation*).

**If you're unsure of the best strategy for yourself**, think about what you naturally do when you feel relaxed—because your nervous system associates those actions with feeling safe. For example, you might hum, stretch, let a long breath out, go outside, or cuddle up with a blanket.

**When you notice that your stress is getting close to the line (or has crossed it) and you take action to reduce it**, you're supporting your ability to stay regulated (or return to regulation in a triggered moment). Depending on your level of stress, it may take more or less time to return to a regulated state. Responding to everyday challenges as your best self may look like…

- calm confidence.
- curiosity about what's triggering your child's behavior.
- holding a boundary with compassion.

- using humor to turn things around.
- getting creative about how to solve a problem.

And thanks to neuroplasticity, as you practice tuning in with your stress level and taking action when needed, this will become more automatic over time.

Also, you will create new associations of safety with experiences that currently fuel stress, making it more likely you can stay regulated in the future. "If we go into whatever calms us over and over and over and over…we're firing our brain for peace so that it wires for peace" (Martha Beck, PhD, Beyond Anxiety).

**But it's not always realistic to show up as the parent you aspire to be—after all, we don't parent in a vacuum.**

- We're dealing with our own stuff.
- We're dealing with our child's stuff.
- We're dealing with our parenting partner's stuff.
- Maybe we're dealing with multiple children's stuff.
- And we're dealing with the stuff happening around us.

**Parenting is not about perfection. Parenting is about growing into our best selves while helping our child do the same.**

# When a Storm Has Passed

Sometimes we can notice when our stress is getting close to the line and take action to reduce it to prevent dysregulation—and sometimes we can't.

> View dysregulation as an opportunity to de-shame, repair, and problem solve.

## DE-SHAME

Shame only serves to escalate stress, which can lead to dysregulation—shutting down our capacity to learn and grow and triggering our instinct to react defensively.

So when you react defensively, instead of shaming yourself, try saying, "It makes sense that I reacted that way since it can be our instinct to lash out, withdraw, or people-please when things are too much."

And regulating our nervous system in a triggered moment can be challenging because it requires us to do the following:

- Have awareness of our instinct to react as our defensive self.
- Control our impulse to react defensively.
- Identify and implement strategies to reduce our stress to support our ability to access our best self.

It's a practice that will last a lifetime.

"It's not about being perfect, it's about being aware" (Dr. Shefali, PhD, author of *The Parenting Map).*

You can make yourself a cup of tea, order a pizza for dinner, and go to bed early.

## REPAIR

If we hurt our child with our words or our body, we can say our own version of "I'm sorry that happened. It's never your fault when I lose control of my behavior because my behavior is always my responsibility, no matter what's happening inside me or around me. I'm still growing into my best self, just like you. Will you forgive me? And can we try again?"

The inevitable conflict in a parent-child relationship can serve to prepare our child for the inevitable conflict they will experience in future relationships. When we respond to losing control of our behavior in this way, we role model:

- self-compassion,

- taking responsibility for our own behavior without blaming others, and
- viewing mistakes as an opportunity to learn and grow.

****A Note about Siblings****

If we regularly react to one child in a defensive way, it can fuel disconnection in their sibling relationships rather than the connection we want to foster. To help repair this, we can communicate a message of compassion. "For some people, controlling their behavior comes more easily, while for others, it's more challenging. We're all different. What comes more easily for you? What's more challenging?"

## PROBLEM SOLVE

We can reflect on the earliest sign that our stress was getting close to the line and what might have helped us reduce it.

**If we continue to react to everyday challenges in a stormy way, we can reflect on what unmet need might be fueling our stress and dysregulation.** Once we identify that unmet need, we can make a plan to meet it or help ourselves tolerate one that can't be met to set ourselves up for success in responding to everyday challenges as our best self.

**If you're unsure what unmet need is fueling your stress and dysregulation, you can consider if you're getting triggered by an unmet need from your past.** Our brain is an association machine, so when we experience something in the present that our brain associates (consciously or unconsciously) with stress from the past, it can trigger our defensive behavior. For example, if your parents reacted to your stormy behavior with judgment and consequences rather than understanding and support, then your brain may (consciously or unconsciously) associate your child's stormy behavior with feeling judged and punished, which can fuel your stress and dysregulation.

**Make sense of your story to heal from the past.** In their book, *The Whole-Brain Child*, Daniel Siegel, MD, and Tina Payne Bryson, PhD, explain that making sense of our story is the best gift we can give to our child because it allows us to break unhealthy patterns. If you want to, and it feels safe to, you can do this for yourself by journaling, speaking with a trusted friend, or working with a therapist.

- Reflect on the facts of your past and how they may be impacting your present to create awareness.
- Reflect on how you feel about the facts in a way that creates distance between you and your emotions, making them feel more manageable.
- Identify a message of resilience, "My parents did not meet my needs in this area, but they did the best they could given their own past experiences. And I can use this awareness to learn and grow."

<u>And then, you can practice offering yourself in the present what you needed in the past.</u>

For example:

- Validate your experience: "This is a hard moment."

- Allow yourself to feel your emotions without judgment: Ask yourself, *"What would I say to a friend in the same situation?"*
- Respond to yourself with compassion when you lose it: "It makes sense that I lost it."

**If you don't know why you struggle with regulation but know your stress is often close to the line or has crossed it,** create time to do something that feels good (by saying no to something that feels bad) because the more time we spend doing things that feel good, the more time we spend in a regulated state. The more time we spend in a regulated state, the further away we get from the line between regulation and dysregulation. The further we get away from *that line, the more it takes to push us over that line. This is a feedback loop that supports nervous system regulation.* "We can heal through the repetition of positive experiences" (Bruce D. Perry MD, PhD, on *The Oprah Podcast).*

These are some types of experiences that, when done repetitively, support healing:

- <u>Relationships</u>: Develop and nurture relationships with yourself and others that provide physical and emotional safety. In your relationship with yourself, you can be your own safe space. In relationships with others, you can seek out people who offer you a safe place. Even short bursts of positive interactions with a colleague, neighbor, the delivery person, someone at the grocery store, or a fellow parent at the playground or a school event have a positive effect on your healing (Oprah Winfrey and Bruce D. Perry MD, PhD, co-authors of *What Happened to You?*).

- <u>Rhythmic movement</u>: Rhythmic movement refers to any type of repeated, patterned motion that follows a steady rhythm or beat. Examples include walking, running, riding a bicycle, skating, swimming, bouncing a ball, jumping on a trampoline, dancing, gymnastics, yoga, rowing, swaying, knitting, and drumming.
- <u>Mindful experiences</u>: Mindful experiences include any activity that engages your full attention in the present moment. Examples include reading, journaling, meditating, making art, acting in a play, playing an instrument, singing, listening to music, writing, taking photographs, making videos, baking, cooking, and spending time being present in nature by slowing down, noticing what's around you, and allowing yourself to be deeply moved or amazed by it.

**If you want professional support,** there are a variety of therapies available including:

- <u>Traditional therapy</u> which focuses on thoughts and feelings.
- <u>Somatic therapy</u> which focuses on the mind-body connection.
- <u>IFS therapy</u> which views the mind as containing different "parts" like a family. Each part has its own role, and the goal is to identify and heal each part to access your core "Self" (best self).

- <u>EMDR therapy</u> which is a method that involves moving your eyes a specific way while you process uncomfortable memories.
- <u>Hypnosis</u> which is a natural, relaxed state of focused attention where the mind is more open to positive suggestions. It can help shift patterns of thought, emotion, or behavior by gently working with the subconscious.

If you feel discouraged, practice noticing when you feel good and allow yourself to fully experience those moments.

# Your Child's Storm Plan

# An Introduction

When our child reacts to everyday challenges in a defensive way, their stormy behavior can look like:

- <u>Lashing out</u>: hitting, kicking, throwing, scratching, biting, pushing, screaming, refusing to cooperate, challenging limits, talking back disrespectfully, or acting overly controlling.
- <u>Withdrawing</u>: running, hiding, avoiding eye contact, turning their body away, or not talking.
- <u>People-pleasing</u>: acting overly agreeable, constantly apologizing, or lying to avoid conflict.

**If your goal is to help your child regulate their nervous system so they can access their best self—while also supporting the brain development and skill-building they'll need to grow into someone who can regulate their own nervous system—traditional tools may not be the most effective choice.**

**Consequences and rewards:** Traditional parenting approaches like consequences and rewards are grounded in the belief that behavior is a choice. When a child makes a "bad" choice, they receive a negative consequence; when they make a "good" choice, they earn a reward. The goal is to teach right from wrong.

However, current neuroscience shows that, in overwhelmed moments, children often lack the nervous system regulation required to control their behavior. The brain development needed for this kind of self-control begins around age three or four—and isn't fully complete until the mid- to late 20s. So even for our tweens and teens (especially our tweens and teens), challenging behavior is often an instinctive response to too much stress at a time when they lack both the neurological maturity and the skills to regulate their nervous system—rather than a conscious choice.

For children who are deeply feeling, sensory-sensitive, have ADHD or ASD, have experienced trauma, or have other individual differences, the ability to regulate their nervous system is even more difficult and takes longer to develop.

<u>When consequences and rewards seem effective</u>, it's because our child is regulated enough in that moment to access their best self and make a deliberate choice to avoid a consequence or earn a reward. So use them when they're helpful, but keep in mind that:

- As children get older, the consequences and rewards will need to become bigger and bigger to remain effective... until one day, they're not.

- They don't help children build the skills needed to control their behavior in triggered moments.

**Calming skills:** First came consequences and rewards; then came teaching calming skills—and expecting our child to use them in a triggered moment.

With our current understanding that—until a child's brain matures and their skills develop—they lack:

- awareness of their instinct to react as their defensive self,
- impulse control to pause their instinctive behavior, and
- the ability to identify and implement stress-reducing strategies,

…it follows logically that expecting a child to use calming skills in a triggered moment is unrealistic.

"It's not our child's responsibility to regulate their nervous system until it's developmentally possible" (Mona Delahooke, PhD, author of *Brain-Body Parenting*).

**An alternative approach to challenging behavior is to move away from assuming the child is misbehaving intentionally and instead respond with curiosity about the underlying causes and the support the child needs.**

"Children will do well if they can" (Ross W. Greene, PhD, author of *The Explosive Child*).

Is their challenging behavior rooted in testing limits? If so, a blend of boundaries and autonomy may be needed. Testing limits is a normal part of development. When our child tests limits, we can hold firm boundaries while also offering autonomy. Creating a boundary means identifying a limit or rule that defines what is acceptable and not acceptable in a relationship, situation, or environment. Holding a boundary means taking action when that boundary is challenged, ignored, or crossed. Autonomy is age-appropriate power and control. If our boundary is a 9:00 p.m. bedtime, we can hold our boundary—in this scenario, that might mean not changing our mind despite protests, pleas, or bargains—and we can also offer our child a sense of power and control by allowing them to design their wind-down routine.

<u>Is their challenging behavior rooted in a lack of impulse control</u>? If so, common sense may be needed. The impulse control needed to resist temptation—not taking extra cookies from the cookie jar or not sneaking downstairs at night to get their iPad—is often beyond a child's developmental stage, even when they understand the difference between right and wrong. This is especially the case for kids for whom impulse control is extra challenging. Instead of punishing our child for not having the brain development to control their impulses, we can take common sense action to set them up for success. If they can't resist the cookies, we can choose not to buy them or we can put them where they can't access them. If they sneak down at night to get their iPad, we can identify a way to make it inaccessible.

<u>Is their challenging behavior rooted in a lack of skills</u>? If so, skill-building may be needed. For example, if their sibling

rivalry stems from a lack of problem-solving skills, we can view challenging behavior as an opportunity to teach effective conflict resolution skills and help them practice them over time. If our teenager comes home after curfew because they didn't know how to say no to their friends, we can use the situation as an opportunity to teach them skills for setting and holding boundaries.

> If your child's challenging behavior is rooted in nervous system dysregulation, *The Storm Plan* may be needed.

Our children are not born with the brain development and skills needed to regulate their nervous system. They rely on us to help them regulate while building the skills they'll need to eventually self-regulate.

# When Skies are Clear

**We want to allow our child to experience manageable stress** because when they stretch themselves outside of their comfort zone, they:

- build their tolerance for stress.
- learn and grow into their best selves.

Manageable stress should feel challenging but doable—with enough support to avoid overwhelm, but not so much that it removes the struggle. This is the zone where stress tolerance, learning, and growth happens.

"When your kid ends up seeing themselves as capable of doing something they didn't previously think they could do, that is one of the best rewards" (Becky Kennedy, PhD, author of *Good Inside*).

Here are some everyday examples:

- <u>For a younger child</u>: getting dressed, tying their shoes, putting on their coat, experiencing boredom, working on a puzzle, doing errands with you or a caretaker, learning to read, learning to swim or ride a bike, going on a ride at an amusement park that stretches them, ordering their own food at a restaurant, and learning how to do various chores around the house may be appropriate challenges.

- <u>For an older child</u>: saving up for a purchase, attending overnight camp, joining a club, learning how to play an instrument, singing in the choir, acting in a play, playing sports, planning and cooking a meal, learning to drive, and getting their first job may be appropriate challenges.

After a challenge:

- <u>Celebrate effort over outcome</u>: When we focus on effort over outcome, we encourage our child to embrace challenges rather than avoid them for fear of failing (commonly known as "perfectionism").
- <u>Build internal motivation</u>: For example, we can say, "How does that feel inside?" rather than praising or rewarding their accomplishment, which creates external motivation.
- <u>Reflect</u>: "What helped you get through the hard part?"

<u>However, we want to get to know our individual child</u>, because an experience that fuels manageable stress in one child may fuel too much stress in another based on individual differences such as stage of development, genetics, and past experiences.

Too much stress can lead to dysregulation—shutting down

their capacity to learn and grow and triggering their instinct to react defensively. Therefore, we want to keep our child's stress in check.

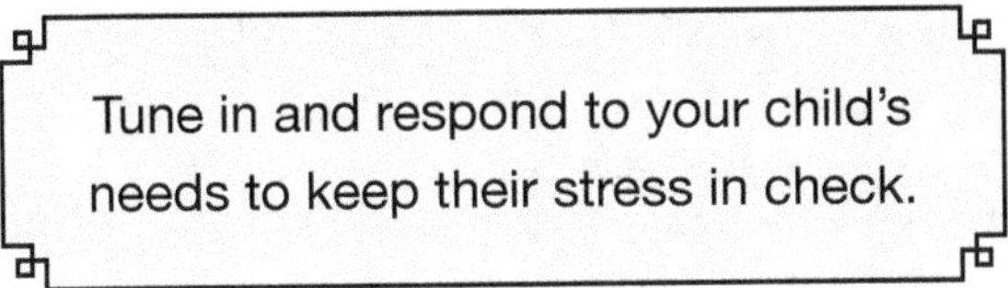


**It's not about tuning in and responding to every need.** It's about creating a balance that allows our child to experience manageable stress so they can build tolerance for it, learn, and grow—while also tuning in and responding to their needs, because:

- Unmet needs can fuel stress and lead to dysregulation, and dysregulation promotes more dysregulation—a vicious cycle,
- Whereas met needs can fuel safety and lead to regulation, and regulation promotes more regulation—a virtuous cycle.

**We can tune in to our child's needs by proactively noticing the signals they send (facial expression, tone of voice, body posture, movement, and gestures) and connecting that information with our knowledge and experience.**

- They're whining and haven't eaten in a while; I wonder if they need food?
- They're taking their clothes off and I just got them dressed; I wonder if the fabric is bothering their skin?

- They're jumping on the couch and we haven't been outside yet today; I wonder if they need movement?
- They are glaring at me and I've been yelling at them; I wonder if they need respect?
- They have been acting withdrawn and haven't been hanging out with their friends recently; I wonder if they need someone to talk to?

When it makes sense to (and when it doesn't trigger our child), we can voice our observations out loud to help them connect their behavior to unmet needs. "We can get really attuned at watching for all forms of expression and wondering and being curious out loud without expectation of any response" (Kelly Mahler, Occupational therapist).

"Many parents see behavior as the measure of who our kids are, rather than using behavior as a clue to what our kids might need" (Becky Kennedy, PhD, author of *Good Inside*).

**We can encourage our child to tune in to their own needs by noticing the clues their body and brain are sending.** For a younger child, we can encourage them to focus on their body sensations; "What is your body telling you about what it needs right now?" For an older child, we can encourage them to expand their awareness to other sensations, thoughts, and emotions over time.

**We can role model tuning in and responding to our own needs.**

- "My body feels restless, I'm going to do some jumping jacks."

- "That music is too loud for my ears, I'm going to turn it down."
- "I feel frustrated, I'm going to take a deep breath."

<u>If we ignore, minimize, or rush to get rid of our child's uncomfortable sensations, thoughts, or emotions without understanding the root cause</u>, we may unintentionally create an association between discomfort and threat. When this happens, our child can grow up to be someone who reacts to their uncomfortable sensations, thoughts, or emotions by lashing out, withdrawing, or pretending everything is ok when it's not.

<u>If we stay present with our child's uncomfortable sensations, thoughts, and emotions with an attitude of curiosity about what they need to support their well-being</u>, we create an association between discomfort and safety. When this happens, our child can grow up to be someone who can do this for themselves.

**Generational wealth is often seen in financial terms, but the most valuable legacy we can pass on is one of well-being.** "How our caregivers respond to us becomes how we in turn respond to ourselves, and this sets the stage for how we respond to our children" (Becky Kennedy, PhD, author of Good Inside).

**Once we tune in with one of our child's needs, we can respond by helping them meet it or by helping them tolerate one that cannot be met.**

These are some of their needs that, when met, help keep their stress in check and support regulation.

- <u>Physiological needs</u>: physical safety and well-being, sleep, nutrition, hydration, movement, sensory comfort, and downtime.
- <u>Psychological needs</u>: emotional safety and well-being, connection (feeling connected to others, themselves, and nature), play, predictability, novelty, autonomy, respect, recognition, personal space, intellectual stimulation, a sense of purpose, and spirituality, as well as <u>less</u> screen time, busyness, news, and negativity.

## PHYSIOLOGICAL NEEDS

The most effective way to help our kids develop healthy habits that keep their stress in check is to foster positive associations around the act of doing the things that benefit them (Tina Payne Bryson, PhD, author together with Daniel Siegel, MD, of *The Power of Showing Up*).

**Physical safety and well-being**

Physical safety is the absence of physical harm.

Physical well-being is the state of having a healthy, functioning body.

**Sleep**

"Sleep is the foundation of our mental health and physical

health and, by extension, our performance in any endeavor" (Andrew Huberman, PhD, host of *The Huberman Lab* podcast).

- Support circadian rhythm adherence by creating opportunities for your child (and yourself!) to view morning sunlight for two to ten minutes early in the day, while the sun is low in the sky, and by minimizing light exposure in the evening (Andrew Huberman).
- Create a regular sleep schedule that allows for an age-appropriate amount of sleep and involves going to bed and waking up at about the same time every day.
- Create a wind-down routine for a younger child that includes a focus on coziness and connection and encourage an older child to create their own wind-down routine.
- Create an environment conducive to sleep: cool, dark, and no electronics.

**Nutrition**

"When 75% or more of the food we consume is from non-processed or minimally processed foods, we're set up to get the nutrients that we need" (Andrew Huberman, PhD, host of *The Huberman Lab* podcast). So, eat real food when you can and let it go when you can't.

Tips from Julie Miller, founder of Three Peaks Education:

- Teach your child that different foods fit into different groups and that our bodies need food from all the food groups.

- Encourage them to listen to their body cues—cues about hunger and fullness and about how they feel after eating different foods.
- Consider having them help plan, shop for, and prepare a meal once a week or once a month.
- For picky eaters, create safety around mealtimes by always offering a preferred food. Also offer new foods and encourage your child to stretch themselves outside of their comfort zone by taking small steps over multiple meals: look, smell, touch, and eventually taste.

We can create positive associations around mealtimes while also helping children stretch themselves to stay at the table longer by reading books to younger children and, for older children, play mealtime games or share stories about our day.

**Hydration**

"When we're dehydrated, our brain and body don't function as well, even if it's slight dehydration" (Andrew Huberman, PhD, host of *The Huberman Lab* podcast). The best way to stay hydrated is by sipping small amounts of water throughout the day and more before and after physical activity and when the weather is hot.

- Role model hydrating throughout the day.
- Provide your child with opportunities to hydrate throughout the day.

**Movement**

Movement lowers stress and elevates mood. Going to the

playground, taking a walk around the neighborhood, and dancing together are great ways to get your young child moving. Older children can be encouraged to identify the ways in which they enjoy moving their body, such as walking, running, yoga, or sports. The important thing is that it be something they choose and that they enjoy doing.

**Sensory comfort**

We experience sensory comfort through soothing sounds, sights, smells, tastes, and textures.

**Downtime**

Relaxation recharges the brain and body. We should note which activities are relaxing for our child and which ones create stress. For example, though screen-free time is ideal, sometimes watching a show or playing a video game can be relaxing for a child. But depending on your child, the show or game, and the amount of time spent watching or playing, these activities can also create stress.

## PSYCHOLOGICAL NEEDS

As parents, we can't control the genes we pass on, but we can try to give our children an environment that will help them make the most of their potential (Laura Markham, PhD, author of *Peaceful Parent, Happy Kids*).

**Emotional safety and well-being**

Emotional safety is safety to express thoughts and feelings

<u>without negative consequences</u> such as being ignored, dismissed, or criticized. When we feel emotionally safe, we feel seen and understood.

<u>Emotional well-being is a person's ability to respond to unpleasant emotions with an attitude of curiosity about what they communicate about their needs</u>. Since thoughts, emotions, and body sensations form an interconnected feedback loop, emotional well-being also involves responding to sensations and thoughts with curiosity about what they communicate about unmet needs.

<u>We can support our child's emotional well-being by:</u>

- Teaching them to identify their emotions.
- Helping them question their thoughts using Byron Katie's method, The Work.
- Caring for their physical needs, including sleep, nutrition, hydration, movement, sensory comfort, and downtime.

<u>Teaching our child to identify emotions is important because this awareness supports their ability to know and meet their needs</u>. For a younger child, we can make an observation, "You seem surprised." As they grow, we can pose our observations as a question to encourage them to identify their own feelings, "You seem angry?" Having a more nuanced vocabulary for emotions will enable them to identify their feelings more accurately (Brené Brown, PhD, MSW, author of *Atlas of the Heart*).

<u>For deeply feeling kids</u>: "Deeply feeling kids tend to hate

talking about their feelings. It feels like too much, too intensive, too intrusive" (Becky Kennedy, PhD, author of *Good Inside*). For these kids, instead of asking how they feel, we can ask if they feel good (thumbs up), okay (thumb in the middle), or bad (thumbs down) to begin building their tolerance for talking about their feelings.

<u>While helping our child identify their emotions, we want to be aware of the difference between "identifying them" and "creating them."</u> For example, when a child experiences something for the first time—such as hearing a loud clap of thunder, going swimming, going to an amusement park, spending the night at a friend's house, or flying on a plane—and looks to us to know how to feel, we can we can respond in ways that help them feel safe and form positive associations with new experiences (Tina Payne Bryson, PhD, author together with Daniel Siegel, MD, of *The Power of Showing Up*).

<u>Role modeling</u>: Role modeling emotions requires nuance. When our child observes our emotions, we don't want to deny them because that can create an association between uncomfortable emotions and threat. Instead, we can acknowledge our feelings in a way that creates safety around them. For example, saying "I feel sad, and I'm still your strong mom who can take care of you" (Becky Kennedy, PhD, author of *Good Inside*) shows our child that emotions are safe and manageable, not dangerous or overwhelming.

The nuance is that we never want to communicate our emotions in a way that makes our child feel responsible for them.

For instance, if our child is being uncooperative and we say, "That makes me feel so frustrated," we may unintentionally teach them that they are responsible for our emotions. In contrast, if we say, "I feel frustrated, so I'm going to take a deep breath to help me respond the way I want to," we are modeling taking responsibility for our emotions.

If our goal is to teach empathy, the most effective way we can do that is to offer it. For example, if our child says, "I hate you!" instead of responding with "That makes me feel so sad—we can say, "You must be really upset to say something like that. Talk to me. I want to understand."

<u>These are some other things we can teach our child about emotions</u>:

- Emotions, even unpleasant ones, are helpful because they communicate information about our needs. When we're unsure what information they communicate, it's okay to give ourselves some time to feel our feelings before deciding what to do about them.
- Emotions can be labeled with words in our mind and felt as sensations in our body.
- We can feel more than one emotion at a time.
- Emotions can be expressed in many ways, including through words, art, or physical activity.
- Emotions are like the weather, they're always changing.

As our child builds awareness of their own emotions and needs, they will build awareness of others' emotions and needs.

# CONNECTION WITH OTHERS, SELF, AND NATURE

**Connection with others:**

**Strengthen connection with your child by spending 1:1 time together:** For younger children, we can spend time together doing something they enjoy such as playing with toys, engaging in imaginary play, coloring or arts and crafts, singing and dancing, reading books, walking or playing outside, exploring nature, or even doing chores together such as cleaning, gardening, or grocery shopping.

For older children, we can spend time together doing something they enjoy such as going for a walk, playing a card, board, or video game, doing a creative activity together, playing catch, shooting hoops, watching a show, asking them questions to get to know them better, baking or cooking, sharing funny videos, looking at photo albums, reading together, or going out to dinner or a movie.

And when we don't have time to spend with them because we're busy working, doing laundry, or making dinner, we can feel reassured that these everyday tasks that put food on the table and clean clothes in their drawers provide cues of safety that support nervous system regulation" (Tina Payne Bryson, PhD, author together with Daniel Siegel, MD, of *The Power of Showing Up*).

**Strengthen connection with your child through communication:** Effective communication has the power to create connection, whereas ineffective communication has the power to create disconnection.

<u>State clear expectations to set your child up for success</u>:

- "Please don't draw on the wall, but you can draw on paper. Do you remember where we keep it?"
- "Please don't jump on the couch, but you can jump on the floor. Show me!"
- "Please don't grab, but you can ask if you can have a turn when they're done. Try it!"
- <u>For an older child</u>: "Please don't talk to me in a way that makes me want to walk away; talk to me in a way that makes me want to listen. I want to understand."

<u>Use humor</u>:

- "Don't get in your car seat; they're just for adults!"
- "It's time to put your shoes on your head! What do you mean they don't go on your head? Where else would you put them??"
- When it's time to leave the playground, "Should we fly like a bird or hop like a bunny?"
- <u>For an older child</u>: "I'm sorry to tell you that the maid is off today… I know it's asking a lot… but could you possibly hang up your coat?"

<u>Offer positive choices</u>:

- "Would you like to wash your hands in the kitchen sink or the bathroom sink?"
- "Would you like to put your shirt or your pants on first?"

- "Can you do it yourself, or do you need help?" If they don't do it themselves, you can say, "I see you need some help," and help your child do what needs to be done, being as gentle and compassionate as possible.
- <u>For an older child</u>: "Would you prefer to take a break or do your homework first?"

<u>Elicit curiosity instead of making demands</u>:

- "When it's snowing outside, what do your feet need?" instead of, "Put your boots on."
- "Where do your blocks go?" instead of, "Put your toys away."
- "What do we put on our toothbrush?" instead of, "Brush your teeth."
- <u>For an older child</u>: "What time did you agree to turn off your video game?"

<u>Encourage them to use their brain to tell their body what to do</u>:

- "Tell your hands it's time to tie your shoes."
- "Tell your feet it's time to walk."
- "Tell your body it's time to sleep."
- <u>For an older child</u>: "Tell your brain it's time to do your homework."

<u>Be specific to set them up for success</u>:

- Instead of saying, "Be a good friend," say, "When your friend arrives, say hello to her at the door and then offer her the choice of two activities."
- <u>For an older child</u>: Instead of, "Go pack your suitcase,"

say, "Pack five shorts, two pants, seven short sleeve shirts, two sweatshirts, seven pairs of underwear, seven pairs of socks, and three pairs of pajamas."

<u>Allow for a balance of safety and reasonable risk:</u>

When it makes sense, we can ask, "What's your plan to keep yourself safe?" instead of automatically saying "No." We can use this strategy whether we're speaking to a younger child at the playground or an older one heading to a party.

<u>Communicate thoughts that assume the best:</u>

The way we speak to ourselves, our child, and people in our world will become the way our child will speak to themselves, to us, and people in their world. When we speak as our defensive self, we teach our child to assume the worst, which fuels threat. When we speak as our best self, we teach them to assume the best, which fuels safety.

<u>Listening:</u>

Effective listening is listening without interrupting and with the intent of understanding the other person's perspective rather than listening with the intent of proving them wrong. After our child is done speaking, if necessary, we can ask follow-up questions to ensure we understand their point of view, and then reflect back what we heard them say so they feel heard.

<u>If you're busy:</u>

If you're unable to listen in the moment, you can say, "Let me just finish what I'm doing and then I can listen because I really want to hear what you have to say."

<u>If you have advice to offer</u>:

You can ask your child, "Do you want some advice, or do you want me to just listen?" As parents, we want our children to benefit from our experience and knowledge. But sometimes our child just wants to talk about their stress to reduce it, not because they need our help solving a problem. If we ask rather than force our opinion on them, they'll be more open to our input when they do need help (William Stixrud, PhD, and Ned Johnson, authors of *What Do You Say?*).

<u>If your child is not listening</u>:

Try getting down to their level, gently touch their shoulder, and acknowledge what's got their attention. For a younger child, you might say, "I see you're playing with your trucks." For an older child, "I see you're on your phone." Then you can say, "I need your attention. Can you look at me?"

**Strengthen connection with your child in adolescence**

An adolescent's job is to separate from their parents and start to form their own identity.

But as they seek to separate from us, we want to understand that they still desperately need us—so we want to have the wherewithal to allow them their space while continuing to prioritize connection, despite the attitude, eye-rolls, and closed doors.

**Strengthen family connections**

Ways that we can strengthen family relationships include planning family activities such as family walks, board games, movie nights, and shared meals to create opportunities to talk, laugh, and learn more about each other. If a daily meal is not realistic, consider a weekly breakfast or dinner together.

**Strengthen friendship connections**

In addition to fostering a sense of belonging and safety, friendships offer our child the opportunity to learn who they are as an individual separate from us. This process can begin as early as age two. Friendships are especially important during adolescence, as they help teens grow in independence and develop a stronger sense of identity.

**Strengthen community connections**

We can help our child develop relationships within their community by spending time with neighbors, participating in community events, volunteering, and supporting local businesses.

**Strengthen connection with themselves**

When our child has quiet opportunities to connect with themselves, it supports their ability to tune in to their body and brain for clues to their needs.

**Strengthen connection with nature**

"When your child spends time in nature, it calms their nervous system, deepens breathing, releases oxytocin, reduces stress, quiets negative self-talk, boosts their immune system, lowers blood pressure, improves sleep, improves mood, and more" (Dacher Keltner, PhD, author of *Awe*). So, encourage your child to play in the dirt, in puddles, and with rocks. Go for nature walks. Watch a sunrise or sunset.

## Play

Play can broadly be defined as time spent doing something you enjoy. "Play and playful states are incompatible with threat states" (Tina Payne Bryson, PhD, author together with Daniel Siegel, MD, of *The Power of The Yes Brain*).

## Predictability

Children flourish when they know what to expect. You can help them by:

- Creating a daily routine.
- Letting them know what to expect and what is expected of them when doing something new.
- Anticipating issues and strategizing ways to set everyone up for success.

## Novelty

Create opportunities for your child to experience new things: take them to new places, do new things, and meet new people.

## Autonomy (with limits)

Age-appropriate power and control is an antidote to stress.

However, for a child, feeling as though they're the one in charge can activate stress. There must be a delicate balance of offering age-appropriate power and control together with communicating and holding boundaries.

**Respect**

Our child is not our equal in terms of experience, but they are our equal in terms of their need and right for respect.

**Recognition**

No matter their age, a child wants to feel recognized for who they are on the inside, not for how they look or what they accomplish. We can notice and communicate what they contribute to our relationship and to the family that is unique and valued.

**Personal space**

Personal space is the physical distance a person needs around them to feel comfortable.

**Intellectual stimulation**

We can support our child's need to learn about the world by encouraging exploration and helping them make sense of it through meaningful conversations that foster critical thinking.

**A sense of purpose**

There are many paths to your purpose in life. Here are three described by Martha Beck, founder of Wayfinder Life Coach Training.

1. <u>The Mended Path</u>: Find a place where you have suffered and have begun to heal—and then help others who are facing a similar challenge to heal as well.
2. <u>The Path of Fascination</u>: Notice what captures your attention without effort. What draws you in naturally may point you toward your purpose.
3. <u>The Path of Mystery</u>: Ask yourself "What is my purpose?" To know what's right for you, tune into your body for clues—what makes your body feel relaxed may be a sign that it's right for you, while what makes it feel tight may signal it's not. You can also connect with your higher power and ask for guidance, and then get very quiet—and listen.

**Spirituality**

"Spirituality is being in connection and communication with your higher power…to connect with your higher power spend time somewhere you feel peaceful" (Dr. Lisa Miller, PhD, author of The Awakened Brain). Your "higher power" is a broad term that can refer to God, the Universe, nature, your higher self, or any concept that feels right to you.

One of the most effective ways to encourage our child to connect with their spirituality is to model our own curiosity and journey to connect with ours.

**These are some things that children need LESS of to support their psychological well-being:**

- <u>Screen time</u>
  The American Academy of Pediatrics suggests no

digital media for babies and toddlers (except video chatting), one hour of screen time per day maximum for children aged two to five, and consistent limits for older children and adolescents. Jonathan Haidt, PhD, author of *The Anxious Generation*, recommends no smart phones before high school and no social media before age 16.

- <u>Busyness</u>
  "It takes courage to rest and play in a culture where exhaustion is seen as a status symbol" (Brené Brown, PhD, author of *The Gifts of Imperfection*).
- <u>Things</u>
  Fewer toys, clothes, and items in general.
- <u>News & negativity</u>
  Most news is not appropriate for young children. Even for older kids, news usually focuses on what's going wrong, which increases stress, so limit it and consider the best way to consume it when you do.

**When we strive to create a balance that allows our child to experience manageable stress—while also tuning in and responding to their needs to keep their stress in check—we set them up for success.**

# When a Storm is Brewing

> Notice when your child's stress gets close to the line (or crosses it) and hold boundaries on their behavior while taking action to lower their stress.

**Turn stormy behavior into best behavior:** Noticing and lowering stress when needed isn't about shielding our child from discomfort. It's about sensing when their stress gets close to the line (or crosses it)—the line between manageable stress, which builds tolerance, learning, and growth, and too much stress, which leads to dysregulation.

When we sense that their stress is close to the line (or has crossed it), we can hold boundaries on their behavior while taking action to lower their stress so they can stay regulated (or return to regulation in a triggered moment).

<u>Consider this</u>. What if you were up at night with your child, then worked all day taking care of them or at your job outside the home? By the time you connect with your partner at the

end of the day, you're on empty and you lash out at them. It would be understandable if they lashed back (or withdrew) since they're probably on empty, too.

But imagine if they sensed that your stress had crossed the line and offered to help you lower it. "I bet you're exhausted. How can I help?"

- Which reaction would lower your stress and turn your stormy behavior into your best behavior?
- Which reaction would fuel your stress and escalate your stormy behavior?

"We enter a new realm of helpful parenting strategies when we come to understand that agitated behaviors reflect a child's vulnerability and a protective flight-or-fight response, not willful disobedience, and signal the child's need for help, not increased discipline" (Mona Delahooke, PhD, author of *Brain-Body Parenting*).

**Support the brain development and skill-building your child will need to grow into someone who can do this for themselves:** In our culture, we value independence so we may worry that if we help our child regulate their nervous system in a triggered moment, they'll become dependent on us to regulate their nervous system in a triggered moment. However, neuroscience shows us that when we notice our child's dysregulation and respond in a way that helps them return to regulation over and over again, this is the most effective way to support the brain development and skill-building they will need to one day do this for themselves.

<u>Brain development</u>: Relational experiences in which a child feels understood and supported are the foundation for healthy brain development. As their brain develops in healthy ways, they will begin to expand their capacity for awareness and impulse control.

<u>Skill-building</u>: The memories your child forms of you helping them lower their stress will serve as a model for doing it themselves. For example, you may start to notice your child asking for help, listening to music, or going outside to regulate.

"Self-regulation is built through attuned relationships" (Mona Delahooke, PhD, author of *Brain-Body Parenting*).

**For some children, the ability to regulate their nervous system will develop at a younger age and for others, it will take longer to develop.** There is no right or wrong; there are individual differences. What comes easily for some is more challenging for others and vice versa.

When we offer our child the individual support they need to grow into the best version of themselves, they will.

## NOTICE WHEN STRESS GETS CLOSE TO THE LINE (OR CROSSES IT)

Different children have different stress thresholds.

We can notice the relationship signals our child sends—such as tone of voice, facial expression, and body posture or movement—as clues to how close they are to their individual stress threshold.

**Clues that our child is in a safe state:**

- <u>Tone of voice</u>: Calm or joyful
- <u>Facial expression</u>: Attentive, happy, playful, content, or relaxed
- <u>Body posture or movement</u>: Alert, cooperative, playful, receptive, open, or peaceful

**Clues that our child's stress may be building:**

- <u>Tone of voice</u>: Aggressive, hostile, argumentative, sad, or disengaged
- <u>Facial expression</u>: Intense, angry, defiant, distant, or blank
- <u>Body posture or movement</u>: Disruptive, hyperactive, disinterested, slow, or frozen

When we sense that their stress is close to the line (or has crossed it), we can take action to lower it to help them stay regulated (or return to regulation in a triggered moment).

## HOLD BOUNDARIES ON BEHAVIOR

Children rely on their parents to create and hold consistent boundaries for them until they're able to identify and hold their own boundaries.

**Compassionate, stage-appropriate boundaries —even when met with protest—reassure our child that we're**

**in charge, so they don't have to be, and that their upset won't overwhelm us.**

<u>That said, giving in to a boundary because our child protests is very different from thoughtfully changing our mind about a boundary.</u> As Dr. Tina Payne Bryson, co-author (with Dr. Daniel Siegel) of *No-Drama Discipline*, explains: "I want my kids to change their minds about things. I want them to be open when they have new information. So, I want to model that, too."

<u>For example, you have a boundary that no music is allowed during homework time because you've always believed that silence is best for focus.</u> Your child tells you: "I work better with music on." But you're skeptical. You assume they're just trying to negotiate their way around the rules to get what they want. You hold the boundary: "No music during homework. It's too distracting."

But then you happen to listen to a podcast that explains how some people actually concentrate better with music. You pause and realize: Maybe they weren't trying to "get away" with something… maybe they were trying to tell me what works for their brain. So, you come back and say: "I actually learned that focus doesn't always look like silence and that music can help some people focus because every brain works a little differently. Let's try it and see how it goes."

This models:

- Curiosity over control
- Respect for individual learning styles

- The ability to adapt when presented with new insight

<u>Another example is when we set a boundary in a moment of our own dysregulation—one that turns out to be unrealistic or reactive.</u> This becomes an opportunity to model that it's okay to reflect and make a different choice when we have more clarity.

This teaches them:

- That boundaries are important, but not rigid
- That even grown-ups make mistakes and can own them
- That changing your mind isn't weakness—it's wisdom

## TAKE ACTION TO LOWER STRESS

Lowering our child's stress supports their ability to stay regulated (or return to regulation in a triggered moment). We can lower their stress by helping them meet a need or tolerate an unmet need.

**Meet a need:** Sometimes we can help our child lower stress by identifying and meeting a need. Maybe they need to move or rest. Maybe they need softer clothing or less visual stimulation. Maybe they need time with us or time alone.

More often, we may not know what our child needs, or we may not be able or willing to meet their needs at that moment. For example, when we say no to a younger child who asks for sugary cereal, or to an older child who asks for a phone, they may experience an unmet need for autonomy—but in those cases, we may not be willing to meet that need because it conflicts with a more essential one.

When we don't know what their needs are, or we're unable or unwilling to meet them, we can help our child tolerate an unmet need to support nervous system regulation.

**Tolerate an unmet need:** Unmet needs fuel stress. Stress fuels unpleasant sensations, thoughts, and emotions. Unpleasant sensations, thoughts, and emotions fuel more stress. More stress fuels unpleasant sensations, thoughts, and emotions. This is a feedback loop which can lead to dysregulation.

We can help our child tolerate unmet needs without getting stuck in a feedback loop by redirecting their focus to a sensation, thought, or emotion that fuels safety rather than stress. For example:

- Internal sensation: "Let's reach our hands up to the ceiling."
- External sensation: Play some music.
- Relationship sensation: Use humor to diffuse the situation.
- Thought: Ask your child what they would say to a friend in the same situation.
- Emotion: Reassure your child, "This doesn't feel good but you're safe" to evoke a feeling of safety.

**Based on genetics and past experiences, each person is unique in what strategies—or combinations of**

**strategies—fuel safety versus stress.** What creates a sense of safety for one person may cause stress for another. There is no "right way" to reduce stress—only what works best for them and their specific situation. Consider the following ideas, along with your own, and create a personalized list of strategies you believe will be helpful. Then, visualize yourself using them.

Depending on their level of stress, some strategies may help a child tolerate an unmet need in a triggered moment, while others may be more effective in a calm moment at a later time.

This way you will be prepared to take action when needed. If your attempt to help them reduce their stress causes it to escalate, try something different or ask them, "What would help you feel better?"

## REDIRECT THEIR FOCUS TO
## AN *INTERNAL SENSATION*

Using internal sensations to reduce stress often requires mature skills. As our child grows, we can introduce age-appropriate strategies. Breath work and movement are two good ones to start with.

**Breath work:**

<u>Role model belly breathing</u>: Take a deep breath down into your belly and let your exhale be longer than your inhale.

<u>For a young child, encourage them to use their breath to calm themselves by making it fun</u>:

- Pretend to smell flowers and then blow out birthday candles.
- Blow bubbles.
- Give a teddy bear a ride on their stomach (the teddy bear goes slowly up and down as they take deep breaths in and long breaths out).

<u>Other activities that mimic breath work include</u>:

- Singing
- Humming
- Whistling

**Movement**: For a very young child, rock them on a rocking chair, dance with them in your arms, or push them on a swing. For an older child, encourage them to touch their toes, stretch their hands up towards the ceiling, stomp their feet, jump, do chair or wall push-ups, get into a yoga pose, or go for a walk together.

**A variation of progressive muscle relaxation**: Encourage them to imagine that their body is a wet noodle.

# REDIRECT THEIR FOCUS TO AN
## *EXTERNAL SENSATION*

**Sound**: Play calming or upbeat music, use a sound machine to play a soothing sound such as birds chirping, read a book to your child, or play an audio book.

**Sight**: Look at photos, a kaleidoscope, or a gel or sand timer.

**Touch**: Offer a massage, a weighted blanket, a body sock, a stuffed animal, play dough, Legos, water or sand play, a fidget toy, a stress ball, or a necklace made to be chewed on.

**Smell**: Offer a scented pillow, a scented blanket, a scented stuffed animal, an item of your clothing, or something your perfume has been sprayed on.

**Taste**: Offer a drink or a snack.

**Multisensory**: Change your location, walk barefoot outside, watch a show together, or spend time with a pet.

# REDIRECT THEIR FOCUS TO A
## *RELATIONSHIP SENSATION*

Encourage your child to use their body language to send themselves signals of safety.

**Smile**

**Maintain a good posture** with a straight back and shoulders rolled back.

**Unfold their arms** and allow themselves to be open to situations.

<u>Use your own body language to send your child signals of safety</u> (as with any communication, how we say it is more important than what we say).

**A supported meltdown:** If your child is having a meltdown and is past the point of return, offer your compassionate presence while doing what's needed to prevent them from hurting anyone or anything with their body or words—including themselves. If you're in a public space, gently guide them to a more private area.

When your child cries intensely, screams, or flails their arms, it's a natural way for their body to release built-up stress. When you remain present as a calm, compassionate witness, it reassures your child that *you are not overwhelmed by their overwhelm*, and that *they are not alone in it*—which creates a sense of safety.

**Verbal comfort:**

- "This is a hard moment and we'll get through it together."
- "You're a good kid having a hard time."
- "Talk to me, I want to understand."
- "I'm here to help."
- "I believe you." (Becky Kennedy, PhD, author of *Good Inside*).

**Non-verbal comfort**: Communicate support through facial expression and body language.

**Physical comfort**: Offer a hug, pat, or squeeze.

**Empathize and Validate**: Empathize by showing that you understand what they're feeling or experiencing. Validate by letting them know their feelings or experience make sense and are okay to have.

**Share a story**: Share a story of when you were a kid and did a similar thing to lower their shame and open them up to learning (Becky Kennedy, PhD, author of *Good Inside*).

**Use humor to diffuse a situation.**

**Notice and communicate what's happening that is good**: "I see you're doing your best in a tough moment."

**Communicate unity**: "We're on the same team."

**Put both of your hands up as a peace offering**: When you do this, it communicates non-verbally that you're an ally, not an enemy.

**Balance**: Balance the intensity of their reaction. For example, when our child is "high and fast" we can go "low and slow" to create balance.

**Mirror**: Match the intensity of their reaction. For example, if they express upset about something that happened to them, we can use our body, voice, or face to respond with equal upset on their behalf.

**Alone time**: If your child wants to be alone and it's safe to be alone, that's okay, as long as it's their choice and not a consequence. But it's important to offer the availability of our presence because, as mammals, it's our nature to seek safety with a trusted caregiver when we feel unsafe. When they yell, "Go away!" they may be communicating their needs, or they may be instinctively lashing out at a time when they need support. Knowing the right way to respond is a matter of getting to know your unique child.

## REDIRECT THEIR FOCUS TO A
### *THOUGHT OR EMOTION*

Using thoughts and emotions to tolerate unmet needs can require mature skills. As our child grows, we can introduce age-appropriate strategies. Here are some to start with:

**Consider if your thoughts are true or false:** Teach your child that thoughts are not facts and help them do *The Work* (Byron Katie, author of *Loving What Is) by asking them the following questions:*

- Is it true?
- Can you absolutely know that it's true?
- How do you feel and act when you have that thought?
- How would you feel and act without that thought?
- Could the opposite thought be true?
- Could the opposite thought be truer than your original thought?

**Mantra:** Encourage your child to say, "I am safe and I am loved."

**Challenge negative self-talk**: Ask your child what they would say to a friend in the same situation.

**Notice and accept your child's emotions**: Communicate non-judgmental awareness and acceptance of your child's emotions without trying to change them.

**Normalize emotions**: "It's okay to feel ____. Everyone feels that way sometimes."

**Reassure your child to evoke a feeling of safety**: "This doesn't feel good but you're safe."

**A strategy by Martha Beck, PhD, author of *Beyond Anxiety*:**

- <u>Ask your child how they're feeling</u>, "Tell me everything!"
- <u>Validate their feelings</u>, "Of course you're feeling that way with what's going on for you!"
- <u>Help them feel better</u>, "How about I wrap you in a blanket and make you a cup of hot cocoa?

**Present moment gratitude:** Ask your child, "What's happening right now that's good?" to evoke a feeling of gratitude.

**Encourage Kindness**: Encourage your child to focus on the feeling of kindness toward themselves and others.

**Visualization:**

- <u>Calm</u>: Invite your child to bring to mind a pleasant image to evoke a feeling of calm. For example, a calm ocean at sunset, a quiet forest path, a cozy fireplace, a flowing stream, a snowy winter landscape, a lush green meadow, majestic mountains, a floating cloud, a peaceful garden, a gentle rainfall, or a starry night.

- <u>Courage</u>: Invite your child to bring to mind a time they acted with courage to reconnect with that emotion.
- <u>Joy</u>: Invite your child to bring to mind a time they felt joy to reconnect with that emotion.

**Here are some real-life examples of how you can hold boundaries on your child's behavior while also lowering their stress to help them respond to everyday challenges as their best self.**

**Examples for a young child:**

- <u>They're screaming in the bath because they don't like the feeling of water on their head</u>: Hold a boundary for hair washing while also lowering their stress. "Try squeezing my hand while I pour the water."
- <u>Your child is having a meltdown because it's time to leave the playground and they don't want to go</u>: Hold a boundary for leaving while also lowering their stress. "I can see you're upset. That makes sense. Can you walk to the car by yourself, or do you need help?" If they can't listen or need help, help them to the car while role modeling deep breathing. Once you get in the car, offer them a cold drink and a snack.
- <u>They're hitting their sibling</u>: If your child is hitting their

sibling, holding a boundary for physical safety may look like "picking the sibling up. It might look like holding the hitting kid's arms down to their side while saying 'I'm holding your arms down because hitting isn't safe.' It might be sliding your body between two angry kids" (*Big Little Feelings*). Once everyone is physically safe, help them lower their stress by role modeling and encouraging everyone to pretend their body is a wet noodle.

- <u>They're so upset they run away</u>: Find them and lower their stress, "You don't have to be alone with your upset. I'm right here with you. Would a hug help?"
- <u>Your child acts like they don't care (or even laughs) when their sibling falls and hurts themselves</u>: If your child lacks compassion, that can be developmentally appropriate. Another possibility is that they feel so much compassion that they're overwhelmed by it and it's triggered their defensive behavior, causing them to withdraw emotionally. Either way, we want to respond in a way that assumes our child is "good inside" (Becky Kennedy, *Good Inside*). For example, we can use movement to help them lower their stress. "Would you run and get bandages?"

**Examples for an older child:**

- <u>They fall apart and you have no idea why</u>: Depending on what would lower your child's stress, offer:
  - Verbal comfort: "I see you're upset. I'm right here with you."

- Non-verbal comfort: Communicate support through facial expression and body language.
- Physical comfort: Offer a hug, pat, or squeeze
- <u>They said something hurtful to their sibling</u>: Hold a boundary for emotional safety by saying, "I'm here to keep everyone safe," and then lower their stress, "You're a good kid having a hard time. Talk to me, I want to understand. We can figure this out in a way that doesn't hurt anybody."
- <u>They won't turn off their iPad</u>: When screen time is almost over, you can give your child a 5-minute warning. If they don't turn off their iPad when you let them know it's time, you can say, "Can you turn it off yourself or do you need some help?" If they don't turn it off, "Ok, I will help." Take the iPad, using as little force as necessary, and then lower their stress by putting your hand on your heart and softening your expression to show them you understand how hard it is.
- <u>They ask you if they can have a phone, and when you say no, they scream "I hate you! You are the worst parent!"</u>: Hold a boundary on no phone and then lower their stress, "I see that you're very upset. That makes sense."
- <u>They lie</u>: Hold a boundary on lying while also lowering their stress, "Let's go for a walk." And while walking, we can assure them that our goal is to create a relationship in which they feel safe enough to let us know when they get it wrong, and that they can trust us to respond with an attitude of compassion and problem solving rather than criticism and consequences.

**When you notice that their stress is getting close to the line (or has crossed it) and you take action to lower it,** you're supporting their ability to stay regulated (or return to regulation in a triggered moment). Depending on their level of stress, it may take more or less time to return to a regulated state. Responding to everyday challenges as their best self may look like:

- crying instead of hitting
- acting calm instead of stormy
- readiness to move on to what's next
- finding the courage to take a step towards something that feels challenging
- telling the truth instead of lying

**** A Note about Siblings ****

If a child reacts to their sibling's defensive behavior with their own defensive behavior, we want to recognize it as a stress response, hold boundaries on their behavior, and help them lower their stress.

Tuning in with your child's stress level and taking action when needed is a powerful way to help them stay regulated (or return to regulation), while also supporting the brain development and skill-building they'll need to one day do this for themselves.

Additionally, it will create new associations of safety with experiences that currently fuel stress, making it more likely they can stay regulated in the future.

**But it's not always realistic to bring out the best in our child while also building their skills:**

- Sometimes the best we can do is regulate our own nervous system.
- Sometimes we'll lose it and the best we can do is apologize and try again.
- "Even if you don't do anything, brain development is still unfolding" (Tina Payne Bryson, PhD, co-author together with Daniel Siegel of *No-Drama Discipline*).

**As our child begins to demonstrate moments of self-regulation, we can expect those moments to be inconsistent as their brain is still developing and their skills are still emerging.** Sometimes they'll be able to regulate their nervous system on their own and sometimes they'll need our help. We can think of ourselves as their coach who is there to support them.

# When a Storm Has Passed

Sometimes we can notice when our child's stress is getting close to the line and take action to reduce it to prevent dysregulation—and sometimes we can't.

> View your child's dysregulation as an opportunity to de-shame, repair, and problem solve.

## DE-SHAME

Shame only serves to escalate stress, which can lead to dysregulation—shutting down our child's capacity to learn and grow and triggering their instinct to react defensively.

So when our child reacts defensively, instead of saying:

- "You always ruin everything when you get upset,"
- "Don't be a baby,"
- Or "What's wrong with you?"

We can de-shame our child by saying, "It makes sense that you reacted that way since it can be our instinct to lash out, withdraw, or people-please when things are too much" (using whatever language makes sense given the circumstances and your child's stage of development).

And regulating their nervous system in a triggered moment can be challenging because until a child's brain matures and their skills develop, they lack:

- awareness of their instinct to react as their defensive self,
- impulse control to pause their instinctive behavior, and
- the ability to identify and implement stress-reducing strategies.

We can reassure our child that they can count on us to support them as they grow into their best self.

## REPAIR

If they broke something or made a mess, using a tone of curiosity and compassion rather than blame and shame, we can ask a younger child, "How can we fix this?" or an older child, "How can you fix this?" If they hurt someone with their body or their words, we can say, "What would you want someone to say or do if this happened to you?"

We don't want to demand they apologize because, when it's forced, it means nothing to the other person and, therefore, does nothing to repair the relationship. Instead, we can take the long view and recognize the most effective way to teach our child to apologize is to role model it ourselves.

## PROBLEM SOLVE

We can reflect on the earliest sign that their stress was getting close to the line and what might have helped them reduce it. Depending on our child's stage of development, we may want to reflect together.

**If our child continues to react to everyday challenges in a stormy way, we can reflect on what unmet need might be fueling their stress and dysregulation.**

- <u>Unmet physiological needs</u>: Does your child tend to react defensively when they're not feeling well? When they don't get enough sleep? When they're hungry or thirsty? When they need more movement or downtime? When they're wearing certain fabrics or dealing with other tactile experiences such as eating or hair washing? When it's too noisy or chaotic? When they're experiencing too much visual stimulation? In reaction to certain smells?

- <u>Unmet psychological needs</u>: Does your child tend to react defensively when they experience unpleasant thoughts or emotions…or when they don't feel safe to express their unpleasant thoughts and emotions? When they feel disconnected from you? When there is conflict with a sibling or friend? When they don't spend enough time in nature? When they don't get enough play time? When they need more predictability or novelty? When they need more power and control? When they need respect or recognition? When they need more personal space? When they spend too much time on their screens, when they're too busy, or when they're exposed to too much news and negativity?

**For example,** if our child refuses to go to school in the morning, we can consider whether the underlying cause might be:

- Physiological — such as exhaustion, hunger, lack of sleep, illness, or sensory overload.
- Psychological — such as anxious feelings related to a social situation, transitions, academic struggles, or a lack of emotional safety in that environment.

**If we aren't sure what's fueling their stress and dysregulation, we can:**

- Keep a journal to look for patterns.
- Engage in pretend play with a younger child because it will often reveal what's on their mind (*The Way of Play* by Tina Payne Bryson, PhD, and Georgie Wisen-Vincent, LMFT).
- Brainstorm together with an older child by saying, "I've noticed ______. What's up?" (This is a collaborative problem-solving approach developed by Ross Greene, PhD, author of *The Explosive Child*.)

**Once we identify the unmet need fueling their stress and dysregulation,** we can make a plan to meet it or help our child tolerate one that can't be met to set them up for success in responding to everyday challenges as their best self.

For children under the age of three, it's appropriate for the parent to identify the plan. For children older than three, it's often still appropriate for the parent to do so.

<u>Sometimes a new boundary is the plan</u>:

- If we think they need more sleep, we can create a new bedtime boundary.
- If we think they need less time on social media, we can create a new screen time boundary.
- If we think they need us to regulate our own nervous system, we can work on that.

<u>Sometimes tweaking our child's environment is the plan</u>:

- If we think they need more downtime (or movement), we can let something go (or add movement in).
- If we think they need more predictability, we can create more routine in their schedule.
- If we think they need more connection with us, we can prioritize one-on-one time with our child.

<u>Sometimes outside support is the plan</u>:

- If we think a medical issue may be the underlying cause of their behavior, we can bring them to their pediatrician for support.
- If we think sensory sensitivities or motor challenges may be the underlying cause, we can ask their

pediatrician about getting support from an occupation-al therapist.

- If we think a challenge at school may be the underlying issue, we can ask their teacher for support.
- If we think unpleasant thoughts and emotions may be the underlying cause, we can support their well-being at home by prioritizing sleep, nutrition, movement, connection, and by limiting screen time and social media. And we can ask their pediatrician about getting support from a therapist. For a child under 10, play therapy is often best. For an older child, we can consider a traditional therapist and we can also consider non-traditional therapy options such as art therapy, music therapy, sound therapy, aromatherapy, animal therapy, nature therapy, yoga, meditation, Reiki, EFT (also known as tapping), EMDR therapy, somatic therapy, and IFS therapy.

<u>Sometimes it's beneficial to encourage our child to identify the plan</u>. "I've worked with 3-year-olds who were better able to participate in a [problem solving] process than 17-year-olds" (Ross Greene, PhD, author of *The Explosive Child*). When we provide our child opportunities to solve problems:

- They learn to be problem solvers.
- We offer age-appropriate power and control, which elicits motivation.
- They're more likely to implement the solution if they identify it.

- They develop communication skills, confidence, and competence.
- We create a culture of connecting rather than disconnecting when there is a problem.

We want to approach our child at a calm and connected time when they are open to talking or schedule a conversation for a time they agree to. And we want to bring the attitude of "me and my child against the problem, rather than me against my child, who is the problem" (Becky Kennedy, PhD, author of *Good Inside*).

## EXAMPLE 1

- **Identify the behavior without judgement:** "I've noticed that when it's your brother's turn to pick the movie, and you don't like his choice, you say hurtful things to him."
- **De-shame:** "It makes sense that you react that way since it can be our instict to lash out when things feel too bad."
- **Encourage your child to imagine what might help them access their best self:** "What would help you express your upset in a way that doesn't hurt anyone's feelings?".
- **Listen to your child's ideas.**
- **If needed, share an idea:** "I wonder if drawing a picture about how you feel would help you express your disappointment without hurting your brother?"

- **Agree on a plan and then encourage your child to identify a signal you can use to remind them of it if needed.**

## EXAMPLE 2

- **Identify the behavior without judgment:** "I've noticed you hide in my arms when it's time to go in the pool for swim class."
- **De-shame:** "It makes sense that you react that way since it can be our instinct to withdraw when things feel too scary."
- **Encourage your child to imagine what might help them access their best self:** "What would help you go in the pool so you can learn to swim—but in a way that feels doable?"
- **Listen to your child's ideas.**
- **If needed, share an idea:** "I wonder if it would help to slow things down and take it step by step? What if, at the next swim class, you sit on my lap and watch the class from a distance? And the following time, you can sit on my lap by the edge of the pool?"
- **Agree on a plan and then encourage your child to identify a signal you can use to remind them of it if needed.**

# EXAMPLE 3

- **Identify the behavior without judgement:** "I noticed you let your sister have her way whenever you two have a disagreement."
- **De-shame:** "It makes sense that you react that way since it can be our instinct to make other people happy to avoid conflict when things feel too big."
- **Encourage your child to imagine what might help them access their best self:** "What would help you communicate your needs to your sister so you can work towards a solution that works for both of you?"
- **Listen to your child's ideas.**
- **If needed, share an idea:** "Would it help to have a family meeting?"
- **Agree on a plan and then encourage your child to identify a signal you can use to remind them of it if needed.**

**If the problem involves siblings or the whole family**, we can have a family meeting to introduce and practice group conflict resolution skills:

- Communicate your feelings and needs in a way that makes the other person want to listen.
- Listen to the other person's feelings and needs with the intent of understanding rather than proving them wrong.
- Work together to identify a solution that everyone can agree to.

Like all meetings, these conflict resolution gatherings are made more enjoyable with a snack or something fun to power the conversation. This also helps create positive associations around conflict resolution.

"The best things in life are on the other side of difficult conversations" (Kwame Christian Esq., M.A., author of *Finding Confidence in Conflict).*

**If the agreed-upon plan doesn't work,** they get to try again.

**If you've ensured your child's primary needs are being met but still don't know what's fueling their stress and dysregulation,** focus on nurturing a relationship with them that offers physical and emotional safety—because safe, connected relationships are the foundation for developing nervous system regulation.

****A Note about Siblings****

If one child's stormy behavior regularly fuels their sibling's stormy behavior, we can make a plan to set them up for success in responding to that challenge as their best self, rather than their defensive self.

**The problem is not our child.** The problem is that our culture expects our child to regulate their nervous system as if they were an adult, even though it is not yet developmentally appropriate for them to do so. In fact, as a culture, we often hold our children to higher standards than we hold ourselves.

Instead, we can expect our children to act like children

because nervous system regulation takes decades to fully develop. And because of individual differences, for some it can be more challenging and take longer.

> We can change our definition of success from "My child is able to regulate their nervous system" to "I'm helping my child regulate their nervous system so that one day they'll be able to do it on their own."

**Stress is inevitable, but when you respond to your child's stormy behavior with understanding and support rather than judgment and consequences—you guide your family in the direction of peace.**

"If you want to improve the world, start by making people feel safer" (Stephen Porges, PhD, author together with Seth Porges, of *The Polyvagal World*).

It's never too early or too late to start parenting differently.

# Conclusion

*The Storm Plan* is a practical, two-part framework designed to help you regulate your unique nervous system and support your children in regulating theirs—so you can show up as the parent you aspire to be and bring out the best in each child, creating more peace in your family.

- When Skies are Clear: Tune in and respond to needs to keep stress in check.
- When a Storm is Brewing: Notice when stress gets close to the line (or crosses it) and hold boundaries on behavior while taking action to reduce stress.
- When a Storm Has Passed: View dysregulation as an opportunity to de-shame, repair, and problem solve.

**If *The Storm Plan* resonates with you,** scan the code below or visit LauraReardonCoaching.com to learn more about The CUSTOMIZED Storm Plan or to inquire about a speaking engagement.

You've got this and I've got you.

# A Note from the Author

Thank you for reading *The Storm Plan*. I hope it will help you create more peace in your family.

As a self-published author, I rely on readers like you to help others discover this book. If you found it helpful, I'd be truly grateful if you'd take a moment to leave a review on Amazon.

Your feedback helps other parents discover *The Storm Plan* — so they can create more peace in their families, too.

Together, we can build a more peaceful world.

With gratitude,
Laura Reardon

# Acknowledgments

**To my husband**, thank you for making it possible for me to do the work that feels most meaningful to me while making sure I get out and have some fun, too.

**To my mother**, who knew I was going to write this book before I did. Thank you for being my biggest fan and for being the person that I could go to every time I needed to figure things out by talking them out.

**To my pets**, my two dogs Jack and Lucy, and my two cats, Shiner and Teddy – thank you for your companionship as I wrote this book. An extra thank you to the dogs for getting me out for a long walk at the end of each day. And a special acknowledgment to Jack, who passed away the day after I finished writing, and to Lucy, for helping me heal.

**To Dr. Mona Delahooke**, thank you for teaching me about the new paradigm in parenting in your Brain-Body Parenting Collective.

**To Dr. Tina Payne Bryson**, thank you for teaching me practical ways to apply neuroscience to everyday parenting challenges during your Office Hours sessions.

**To Dr. Martha Beck,** thank you for teaching me how to access my internal compass in The Wayfinder Compass training.

**To Cecilia and Jason Hilkey,** thank you for inspiring me to walk on skinny branches in your Happily Family Parent Coach Training Program.

**To Sharyn Timerman,** thank you for your Child Behavior Certification Program; the knowledge I gained serves as the foundation of my work.

**To Laura Bissell,** thank you for editing my book and making me look like a better writer than I am.

**To my PCC mastermind group and my CC mastermind group,** thank you for helping me figure things out along the way.

**To My Library Group,** thank you for being the original supporters of Laura Reardon Coaching.